B EFORE the castle was built, the River Conwy, separating the high mountains of Snowdonia from the gentler hills of Clywd to the east, had formed an obstacle to would-be attackers and a defence for the men of Gwynedd for thousands of years. Conwy, a name at least two thousand years old, is from a Celtic word meaning 'reedy, rushy' and these grasses still grow in profusion along her banks.

Many of the hills overlooking the river have the remains of the forts of Celtic iron-age chiefs. In A.D. 79 they were defeated by the Romans, who built a fortress 5km upstream from Conwy at Caerhun — *Canovium* — where only a few humps and bumps in a field remain of its once formidable defences.

As Roman power dwindled away, Welsh princes took up the reins of authority and, a thousand years after the Romans built their fort at Caerhun, Llywelyn the Great, Lord of Snowdonia, gave Conwy to the Church . . .

1197

He granted lands in Conwy for Cistercian monks to build an abbey. Much of the area of the present town would once have been occupied by monastic buildings. But in the winter of 1282, after two fiercely fought wars, between his descendent, Llywelyn ap Gruffudd, and the English King Edward I for the overlordship of the Principality of Wales, Llywelyn was killed and his army routed.

King Edward I, the English king, set about defending his newly-won principality with a series of stupendous fortresses with defended towns alongside. Conwy is taken by many to be incomparably the most magnificent of them. But all was not easy, and in March 1283 the King's master architect, James of St. George, reported to the King in the Abbey of Aberconwy...

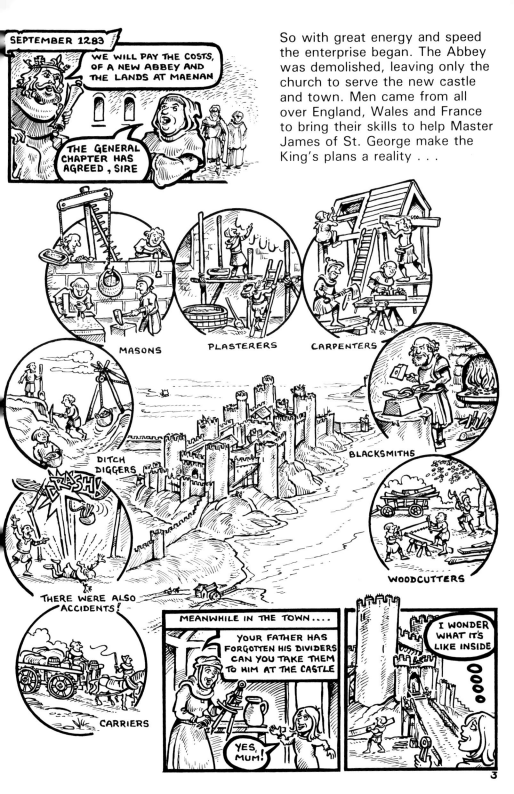

So with great energy and speed the enterprise began. The Abbey was demolished, leaving only the church to serve the new castle and town. Men came from all over England, Wales and France to bring their skills to help Master James of St. George make the King's plans a reality . . .

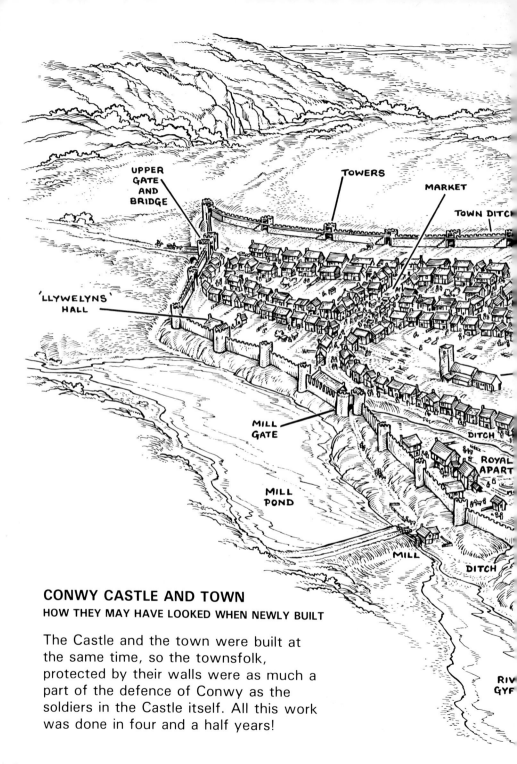

UPPER
GATE
AND
BRIDGE

TOWERS

MARKET

TOWN DITCH

'LLYWELYNS'
HALL

MILL
GATE

DITCH

ROYAL
APART

MILL
POND

MILL

DITCH

RIV
GYF

CONWY CASTLE AND TOWN
HOW THEY MAY HAVE LOOKED WHEN NEWLY BUILT

The Castle and the town were built at
the same time, so the townsfolk,
protected by their walls were as much a
part of the defence of Conwy as the
soldiers in the Castle itself. All this work
was done in four and a half years!

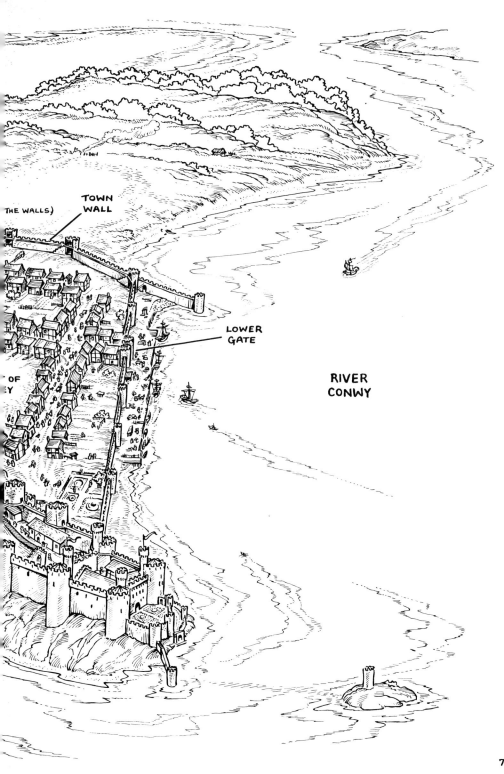

THE WALLS)

TOWN
WALL

OF
Y

LOWER
GATE

RIVER
CONWY

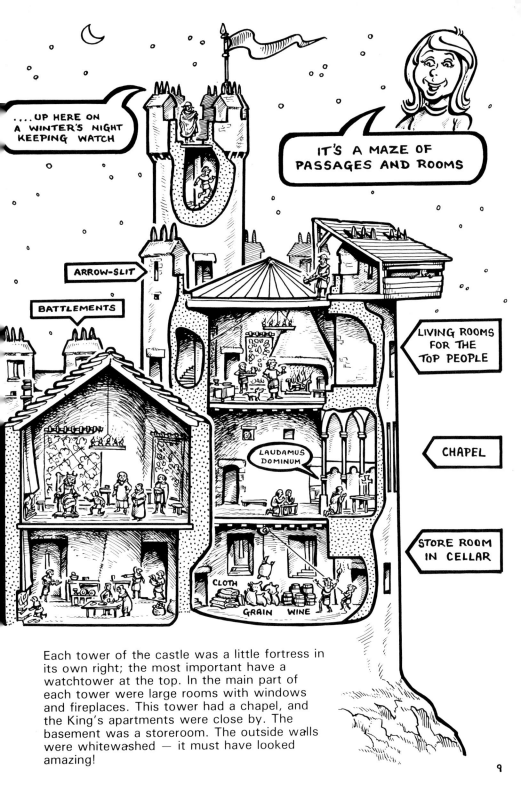

Each tower of the castle was a little fortress in its own right; the most important have a watchtower at the top. In the main part of each tower were large rooms with windows and fireplaces. This tower had a chapel, and the King's apartments were close by. The basement was a storeroom. The outside walls were whitewashed — it must have looked amazing!

Write **your** answers here

(1) . . . .   (6) . . . .

(2) . . . .   (7) . . . .

(3) . . . .   (8) . . . .

(4) . . . .   (9) . . . .

(5) . . . .   (10) . . . .